Ayatollah Sayed Muhammad al-Shirazi

If Islam were to be established in Iraq

Translated by
Z. Olyabek

*Published by Yasin Publications with
the permission of*
Imam Shirazi World Foundation
1220 L. Street N.W. Suite # 100 – 333
Washington, D.C. 20005 – 4018,
U.S.A.
www.TheGrandAyatollah.com
English edition

Content

Translator's Foreword

Not a single one of the governments in the 55 Muslim countries today has implemented an Islamic system of government. Some of these governments may claim to practice Islam but in reality that is about as far as they would go in this respect. Of course the Muslim people in various countries aspire to see a truly Islamic system of government established. In some countries with a predominantly Muslim population, Islamist activists have managed to form an effective opposition to the ruling governments. Such oppositions offer an alternative based on the teaching of Islam to the status quo. In some Muslim countries there is conflict between the Muslim activists who want to see a system of government of their choice, preferably that based on the teachings of Islam, and others who have imposed their own system of government.

One of the main causes of these difficulties is the ignorance of Islam's teachings. On the one hand, when some Muslims attempt to implement Islam, because of their incorrect and incomplete understanding of the teachings of Islam, they do not succeed to implement a system that is intended by Islam. In fact in that way they manage to distort the picture of Islam.

On the other hand, there is also a systematic stereotyping against Islam and Muslims and a relentless campaign to distort the image and the teachings of Islam.

As a result, the misconception has developed which portrays Islam as a system of violence, intolerance, denial of women's right, and the list goes on. Whereas on the contrary Islam stresses non-violence, tolerance, safeguarding women's right in particular and human right in general to an extent that is not available under any other system in the world today.

In this book the author presents the teachings of Islam in a brief and simple manner. This book particularly addresses those Islamists who have created an effective and viable opposition to the ruling system in their countries. It is also anticipated that this book would outline the approach that should be taken by those Muslims who are striving to establish a system of their choice.

When correct teachings of Islam are suitably implemented, this will not only result in the desired outcome, but it will also show others - primarily the non-Muslims - the truth about Islam. It is an unfortunate fact that incorrect and un-Islamic practices by Muslims are usually reflected as being the 'teachings' of Islam.

If one wants to see the real Islam in action, one should consider the practices of the Messenger of Allah, Muhammad peace be upon him, when he formed a true Islamic government.

The book outlines the fundamental aspects of government according to the teachings of Islam, and the policies that a newly established Islamic government need to take if it were to establish an Islamic system of government. The book would also serve as a yardstick for anyone to check the practices of any government that claims to have implemented an Islamic system of government.

Originally written in Arabic, the title of the book was *"If Islam were to be established in Iraq"*. The book was translated since it was considered that its argument is applicable for people who wish to implement Islam in any other country.

In this book, the author emphasises on some of the most important aspects of government such as:

- "System of Consultation for Leadership" that is supported by constitutional establishments,
- Multi-party pluralism,
- Freedoms (such as freedom of belief, thought, expression, education),
- Non-Violence,
- Revival of the single Muslim Ommah,
- Economic self-sufficiency, . . . all within the framework defined by Islam.

The author discusses the issues raised in this brief outline in details in many of his other books. In his works the author emphasises the necessity of adherence to all the teachings of Islam as a complete system and failure to comply with some of the Islamic laws in some aspects would fail to give the desired outcome in the long run. This is because the various issues in life are inter-related and the teachings of Islam are also based on the same system. Therefore any deviations from the teachings of Islam in one respect would inevitably result in failing in another.

Islam defines a set of teachings within a framework that is in harmony with the human nature, as referred to in the Qur'an: *" . . . the original nature according to which Allah fashioned mankind."*[1]

It is for such reasons that make the Islamic laws dynamic and vigorous since they are in total harmony with man's needs.

Adherence to Islamic laws can only be beneficial to mankind, while if he opts out of these laws he would simply lose out. To use an analogy, if someone refuses to obey the physical laws of nature, he will have to face the consequences in the short or long term. For example, if he refuses to accept that boiling water could seriously endanger his health, and immerses his hand in it, then he would have to face the consequences of his refusal. The same applies to compliance with Islamic laws, which affect mankind in various domains, such as personal, social, political, economical.

Therefore if there are any restrictions in Islamic law, they are in the same way similar to the requirement to comply with the physical laws of nature, which are, normally, totally adhered to by mankind.

The author addresses the issue of government as well as other related issues in a number of his books. For more in depth insight into the teachings of Islam on the issue of government, the reader is referred to the author's work some of which are:

1.	Government in Islam,	volume 99 of the *al-Fiqh* series.
2.	The Rights,	volume 100 of the *al-Fiqh* series.
3.	Islamic Government,	volumes 101-102 of the *al-Fiqh*.
4.	Politics,	volumes 105-106 of the *al-Fiqh*.
5.	Economics,	volumes 107-108 of the *al-Fiqh*.
6.	Society,	volumes 109-110 of the *al-Fiqh*.
7.	Peace,	volume 135 of the *al-Fiqh* series.
8.	Freedoms,	volume 139 of the *al-Fiqh* series.
9.	Law,	volume 140 of the *al-Fiqh* series.
10.	The Path of Salvation,	volume 150 of the *al-Fiqh* series.
11.	Leaders of Islam: the Prophet of Islam in Makkah and Medina	

---

[1] The holy Qur'an: the Greek [30]: 30.

Finally the translator wishes to express his gratitude to friends and colleagues for their contribution to the task of translating this book.

Words or sentences within brackets ( ), as well as explanatory footnotes, are added by the translator for clarification.

Z. Olyabek

February 2003

Preface

Praise be to the Lord of the worlds and Blessing and Peace be upon the noblest Messenger of Allah, Muhammad and his amiable and pure progeny, and the anathema of Allah be upon their enemies.

When Islam was first established (as a system), the most important factor that attracted people to Islam was the values it upheld and the respect, facility and help it gave to mankind. For this reason, the Messenger of Allah, Muhammad - peace be upon him and his infallible descendants (S)[2] - needed only to introduce the concept of Islam and practice it. This was the secret of Islam's rapid and enormous progress. In fact, when Makkah surrendered to the Messenger of Allah (S), he forgave all (those who had fought him). Along with the rest of the Muslims, he did not reclaim the houses (and businesses) that had been usurped by the pagans after they had been forced out of Makkah. Instead they lived in tents they erected in the desert. Needless to say, until it surrendered to the Messenger of Allah, Makkah was the capital of the pagans and the idolaters. It was the centre of the force behind all the hot and cold wars planned and executed against the Messenger of Allah (S).

Such conduct, in addition to many others, such as non-violence, good manners, etc. were amongst the best ingredients contributing to the stability and good reputation of Islam. That is why, to secure the stability of the capital of paganism after conquering it, the Messenger of Allah (S) did not have to create an army or a police force, nor other forms of security forces for Makkah. The people of Makkah turned out to be its own guardians and assistants by practicing Islam. They turned out to be some of Islam's greatest supporters after being its staunchest enemies. The Messenger of Allah (S) appointed only one person from the people of Makkah to act as its governor and set a limited salary for him to live on as an ordinary citizen. The

---

[2] It is a mark of piety in Islam to use this salutation (sall-allah alayhi wa aalih) when mentioning the name of the holy Prophet Muhammad.

1

Messenger of Allah, (S), had a similar policy for every district or tribe that accepted his message. This is in addition to the fact that the Messenger of Allah, (S), lived simply throughout his sacred life, before and after his prophet-hood and throughout his life as a statesman, until he died. Because of his simple life style, people used to say about him, *"He lived amongst us like one of us"*. He used to be kind to his enemies in accordance to Allah's recommendation in the holy Qur'an:

Allah forbids you not, with regard to those who fight you not for (your) Faith nor drive you out of your homes, from dealing kindly and justly with them: for Allah loves those who are just.[3]

Equally he used to be kind to Muslims in accordance to the statement of Allah in the Qur'an:

It is part of the Mercy of Allah that you deal gently with them. Had you been severe or harsh-hearted, they would have broken away from around you ...[4] and

Now has come unto you a Messenger from amongst yourselves: it grieves him that you should perish: he is ardently anxious over you: to the Believers he is most kind and merciful.[5]

So, too, were the policies of *Amir_ol_Mu'meneen* (the Commander of the Faithful), Imam Ali[6].

If, by the will of Allah the Almighty, Islam were to be established again, the same policies that were adopted by the Messenger of Allah, (S), must be implemented in government - taking into account

---

[3] The holy Qur'an: The Tested (Woman) [60]: 8.
[4] The holy Qur'an: The Family of 'Emran [3]: 159.
[5] The holy Qur'an: Repentance [9]: 128.
For more details about the way of life of the noblest Messenger of Allah of Islam (S) see:
"For the First time in the History of the World", *"Aromatic Bouquet"*, *"The Aromatic Tradition"*, . . . by the author.
[6] See *"The Islamic Government During the Reign of Amir_ul_Mo'meneen"*, and
"The Governments of the Messenger of Allah and Amir_ul_Mo'meneen" by the author.

the time factor. It is also necessary for rulers to practice what Imam Ali peace be upon him (A)[7] said:

Whoever wants to follow a policy, let him follow the Tradition of his Prophet (Muhammad (S)) otherwise he should not feel safe from doom.

Therefore, if the policies of the Messenger of Allah (S) are practiced, Islam will flourish and Muslims will progress and prosper just as they did during the time of the Messenger of Allah (S). Otherwise Islam would not be safe from falling into disrepute and its position waning to an extent that no Muslim, or anyone who loves the truth, would ever wish to see.

This book, *"If Islam were to be established in Iraq"* is an outline of some of the policies adopted from the noble Tradition of the holy Messenger of Allah, Muhammad (S), taking into account the time factor.

May Allah awaken the rulers to implement the policies of the Messenger of Allah so that Muslims prosper in this world and in the hereafter; surely Allah is the Facilitator and the Helper.

Muhammad Shirazi

Holy City of Qum

1st Rabee' II, 1415 Hejri (1995)

---

[7] It is also a mark of piety to use the salutation *alayhi-salam* (peace be upon him) on mentioning one of the prophets or one of the Imams of the household of the prophet Muhammad.

1

Preventing Bloodshed

Bloodshed inevitably leads to the destruction and downfall of a government. The Messenger of Allah (S) is quoted as saying:

Anyone who aids in the murder of a Muslim, even by uttering a single word, will arrive on the day of Judgement with the phrase "Despondent from the Mercy of Allah" written between his eyes.

The reverse countdown to the downfall of a system of government begins when it delves in the murder and bloodshed of the people. People cannot tolerate the murder of their sons, brothers, sisters, fathers, relatives and friends, etc. They will pick its faults and errors and aim for its downfall. They will denounce its authority and turn public opinion against the regime. A regime that does not rely on the backing of the masses loses the mandate for staying in power.

The downfall of a ruler whose hands are stained with the blood of his subjects, begins with an odd killing here and a murder there, until such killings accumulate and lead to his downfall. Especially if the regime was founded upon the murder of individuals under the pretext that one belongs to a particular rival group, or an opposing political party or a religious sect. The regime may even attempt to eliminate its opponents through false accusations such as arms or drug trafficking charges, and subjecting them to mock show trials under the banner of law, which give the impression of being legal and protecting the state security. Through such illusionary practices, the regime aims to strengthen its position in power. Clearly, this is one of the greatest factors in the downfall of governments, since a government needs the greatest amount of popular support and legal authority to survive.

If such support is not at the government's disposal then not only would it be heading towards a downfall, but also its supporters will ultimately become part of the opposition.

I have seen many governments, and history shows us many others, that had the potential to reign hundreds of years, but they survived only a few years because of their murderous campaign against the people.

The Messenger of Allah, Muhammad (S), did not kill even the murderer of his most beloved uncle Hamzah nor the murderer of his daughter Zaynab along with her child. This was not because they did not deserve to be killed, but for reasons mentioned earlier.

Also Imam Ali (A) forgave all the war criminals taken prisoners during the three battles he engaged in during his reign. Are these not great lessons for those who want to establish Islam?

If, on the other hand, the (newly established Islamic) government was compelled to use force in order to implement the rule of law, it is imperative that that does not surpass imprisonment in the specific cases, which are very few indeed, and some simple fines. This of course must be prescribed through the legal and humanitarian courts of law, which provide all the guarantees necessary to carry out justice.[8]

In this way, a criminal may be prevented from carrying out activities without defiling a revolution with blood.

Other factors, which weaken a government, are practices like torturing and terrorising the people, confiscating their wealth and properties, disseminating false accusations, or even personal sleaze, slander and scandals, etc.

---

[8] For more details in this respect see *al-Fiqh* series, vol. 100, *"Rights"* and *al-Fiqh* series, vols. 101-102, *"Islamic Government"* by the author.

2

General Amnesty

It is imperative for the newly established Islamic government to announce general amnesty for anyone who has committed a crime before the advent of the Islamic government. This is of utmost importance, from one viewpoint, and of immense difficulty from another.

A general amnesty gives reassurance to people about (the intentions of) the new government. In turn, this act would secure their co-operation with the new government. It would lead to stability and security at a time when the government direly needs widespread support and co-operation from the masses. We see that the Messenger of Allah (S) announced amnesty for the people of Makkah. Similarly, *Amir_ol_Mu'meneen*, Ali (A) pardoned the people of Basra and the people of Nahrawan when he overcame their rebellion.

Non-forgiveness will lead to untold difficulties for the new government as the killing and prosecution will not be confined to one place, but will spread to larger areas, just as ripples propagate on the surface of water. In addition, a consequence of not forgiving is confiscation of wealth. Both killing and confiscation generate enemies who sometimes manage to topple a new government as we have seen in many countries.

Furthermore, non-forgiveness incites unrest throughout the country. This results in the loss of the government's valour and reputation and subsequently in its failure. Allah states in the Qur'an:

. . and fall into no disputes, lest you lose heart and your power depart . . .[9]

If the agencies of the young government become embroiled in killing, confiscation and animosity, it would provoke its opponents

---

[9] The holy Qur'an: The Public Estate [8]: 46.

and encourage them to open old wounds and to engage in activities against the government. This would lead the government into more and more troubles, at a time when the new government should be engaged in tackling the country's old problems and not creating new ones that prevent it from developing the country.

The general amnesty is a fundamental principle and if there is to be an exception, it is imperative that measures are taken accordingly as and when absolutely necessary.

3

Good Reputation

Usually an individual wants to live in a society with a good reputation. If an individual, whether a public figure such as a leader or an ordinary person such as a businessman, loses his good reputation, people would at least distance themselves from the individual, if not remove him from his position.

Similarly, a group or an organisation has the same fate as an individual. If a government loses its reputation and people lose their confidence in it, the government would fall and be replaced by another one under a democratic system. In an undemocratic system, however, the government would fall through a popular uprising and suchlike, as we have seen with despotic regimes throughout history.

The use of arms, secret service and false propaganda would be of little help to save the government from falling.

Imam Ali (A) said: *"The opinion-minded person is doomed."*

Reason ensures the continuity of life and if mankind - whether an individual or a group - replaces reason with dogmatic attitude, sooner or later this will lead to the destruction of the individual or the group concerned. It is incumbent, therefore, upon the new Islamic government to ensure that its good reputation remains untarnished. This may not be possible unless the government relies on consultative system and remains popular, humble, of service to the people and adheres to Islamic jurisdiction. The Muslim masses - who are the overwhelming majority in Muslim countries - would not tolerate even a civil servant who does not adhere to Islamic law, let alone a head of state.

The head of state or for that matter, any individual serving in the government should not assume that he could disregard major or minor Islamic legislation even covertly since the Almighty has stated:

And say: "Work (righteousness): soon will Allah observe your work, and His Messenger, and the Believers . . ."[10]

---

[10] The holy Qur'an: Repentance [9]: 105.

4

Action before Slogan

Decent members of society are generally dismayed by hollow slogans. More often than not, dishonest and scurrilous individuals use slogans that are offensive to others. It is therefore important to avoid the use of any slogans, except when absolutely necessary. Adherence to empty slogans might be considered to be useful in the short term, but in fact it is harmful since it distracts the attention and focus from the essence of deed to mere words. Moreover its effect is temporary and would not last long.

The slogan of a successful Islamic party used to be: *"work and do not talk."* The party thus managed to free its country from the grip of colonial powers that had lasted more than a century.

Some of those who look at short-term objectives align their policies with slogans, but do not take any action in line with the slogans. However, responsible individuals follow the agenda that is logically and rationally planned and studied.

Imam Sadiq (A) has said, when addressing his followers:

"Invite people (to Islam) without the use of your tongues."[11] So 'deed' and 'action' is the measure of life, not just mere 'words'.

Slogans usually exaggerate facts more than reality, which could prove counter-productive. For example if you claimed to have established a hundred organisations (to provide services to the community) whereas in reality you have only ninety, people would doubt your accomplishment and deny even the ninety organisations you have established.

However, if you kept a low profile and concentrated your efforts on your activities and improving your performance, people would trust

---

[11] That is you should invite them to Islam through your conduct and behaviour.

you and would appreciate your achievement greatly. People trust a hardworking individual who keeps quiet and credit him with more than his dues, whereas they tend to suspect the one who boasts about his activities. They would credit him less than his dues and may even deny his deed even if he had truly achieved.

It is therefore important that the deed of a person (or an organisation) is more than just words. Action should not even equal words, let alone be less. Slogan is words whereas reality is the deed.

For this reason, it said that one should be prepared for his enemy in two situations:

- First if his adversary observes him doing something with a worrying outcome.

- Second if he is sabre rattling i.e. if he is making claims greater than his capacity and reality, because this means he is heading in the wrong direction.

One problem with slogans is that it attracts the greed and temptation of friends whereas the person who makes such claims is more often than not, unable to fulfil their demands. As a result he loses even their friendship. Furthermore, slogans provoke the enemy since making great claims directs the attention (of others) to the person making the claim and the enemies would assume that he has great resources based on the claims he makes.

Therefore, on the basis of his claims, friends expect more from him while foes are provoked to destroy or incapacitate him so that he does not gain the upper hand.

5

Constitution

The constitution and law in an Islamic system of government differ from those in democratic countries. The constitution in the Islamic system is based on the noble Qur'an, the sacred Teachings of the Messenger of Allah, Muhammad (S), Consensus of religious scholars and Reason.

Unlike the rigidity that the constitution has in some countries, in an Islamic system of government the constitution varies according to the continuous legislation that evolves in light of new developments based on the Teachings of the Qur'an and the Messenger of Allah. The legislation is inferred by the scholars of the 'Council of Jurists' who are chosen by people as their religious authorities at regular intervals, generation after generation.

There have been many circumstances where the 'rigid' constitution written twenty years before was not in harmony with the developments of the day, which in turn causes severe fundamental crisis and socio-political shortfalls. As for the Islamic constitution however, it is able to cope and proceed with all new developments.

Under the Islamic system, the religious scholars or jurists legislate on the basis of the Teachings of the noble Qur'an and the holy Messenger of Allah. The jurists from all schools of Islamic Jurisprudence are the reference and authority for all Muslims following their own school of Jurisprudence.

Therefore, there is no constitution in Islam, as it is formally known, but what we have are the four sources: the Book (the Qur'an), the Sunnah (the Teaching of the Messenger of Allah, Muhammad (S), Consensus (of the jurists) and Reason.

In fact, the advent of constitution in Muslim countries is only since the colonial powers entered those countries. It is befitting to note that Britain, which was behind the creation of constitutions in Iran and Turkey, does not have a fixed constitution as such, but follows what is known as a "constitutional understanding".

They introduced the constitution in the Muslim countries in order to stop the wheel of progress in those countries and hold them back. In doing so they replaced the four references with restrictive and stagnant laws, which brought about the shackling of the Islamic society and its people.

For example the *'Mashroutah'* freedom movement in Iran, which was led by religious scholars, was derailed by the British in order to eliminate the Russian influence and establish control in Iran to their advantage. So by introducing the idea of this constitution, which serves their interests, they brought despots such as the Shah and Ataturk to power in these two Muslim countries and shackled their religion and their worldly fortunes.

Such a stagnant constitution will be problematic from both a legal and rational viewpoint. If we consider a scenario where 100 jurists legislated a law, but after their death people do have the option to follow other qualified jurists. What legal or rational justification is there to adhere to the law, which is considered the constitution, when a majority of the jurists alive hold an opposite view?

Under Islamic jurisdiction, it is the opinion of the jurists who are alive that must be followed for issues of 'new developments' and for those who want to follow a jurist anew.

Rationally, what necessitates a person alive to follow laws legislated by the dead? If it is argued: because it is in accordance with the Book and the Sunnah, the reply would be: Why the go between? Let the Muslims refer (directly) to the Book and Sunnah.

It may be asked: What will the laws be based on? The reply would be, the laws would be based on the treatises of qualified jurists otherwise known as *"Islamic laws"* Journals. Of course the ideal way of implementing that is the creation of 'Council of Jurists' through election of the jurists by the nation[12].

---

[12] For detailed discussion on this topic see *"Consultation (Shura) in Islam"*, *"al-Fiqh* series, vols. 105-106 *'Politics '"*, *"al-Fiqh* series, *'The Path of Salvation '"* by the author and *"Council of the Jurists"* by Murtadha Shirazi.

6

Gradual Implementation

The Messenger of Allah, Muhammad (S), implemented Islam in a gradual way even though Islamic Jurisprudence was complete. The noble Qur'an, in its entirety was first revealed to the Messenger of Allah on a single occasion and later verse-after-verse in accordance with the events of the day.

But if it was possible (for us) to implement Islam 'in one go', we should do so, and we may not resort to the gradual implementation carried out at the time of the Messenger of Allah (S). The revelation was complete before the death of the Messenger of Allah, (S), as Allah the Almighty states:

This day have I perfected your religion for you, completed My favour upon you, and have chosen for you Islam as your religion.[13]

But I am of the opinion that the implementation must be gradual if an Islamic government were to be established in any country, since it would be impossible to do so otherwise given current circumstances.

It is therefore imperative to adopt a policy of gradual implementation where possible so that it does not bring about disorder in society, which could inadvertently result in destruction, harm and other difficulties. In any case, the possibility of implementation (of any aspect of Islam) must be studied on the basis of the principle of *"priorities"*.

It is therefore incumbent upon the newly established Islamic government to create different committees consisting of Muslim jurists and experts of various fields to define the priorities in the process of implementation. This is to avoid any disturbance in the economy, politics, society, management and any other unwelcome outcome.

---

[13] The holy Qur'an, The Table Spread [4]: 3.

For example, if it was decided to change the usury-based banking system to a system based on the *Mudahrabah*[14] system, and the government announced the annulment of all kinds of interest at once - say in a week - one of two consequences could follow:

- Either the government would ban people from withdrawing their assets from banks in which case it will result in chaos and disorder and ultimately, the downfall of the government. Such action is, of course, contrary to the principle *"People have dominion over their wealth".*[15]

- Or the government would not ban the people from withdrawing their assets, in which case it would result in all the wealth and assets being drained from the country's banks. This in turn would result in the collapse of the banking system and high inflation that would seriously harm the poor, the various ongoing projects and people's income.

All of this would reflect upon the stature of the new Islamic government, and people would begin wondering whether the previous regime was a better one. This distorts the reputation of Islam in the eye of the people and leads them to think that the western model is superior to that proposed by Islam.

Similar considerations must be taken into account for other laws of the country.

Therefore it is important that gradual implementation (of Islamic laws) is carried out according to detailed studies of the various committees, which consist of Muslim jurists and experts of respective fields in co-operation with different organisations.

---

[14] *Mudahrabah* is referred to a business investment program where one party provides the capital and the other the business expertise. The parties share the profits and losses of the initiative as defined by the *Mudahrabah* regulations. M. Shirazi, "Islamic Queries", pages 518-519, cases 2283-2289.

[15] The Messenger of Allah has stated this principle.

7

Dynamic Laws

All the laws of Islam are vigorous and spirited because they are legislation from a Powerful, Merciful and Wise deity who is Encompassing and Conversant with all aspects (of mankind) - personal, social, mental and physical, present and future characteristics . . . Allah the Almighty states:

"O you who believe! Give your response to Allah and His Messenger, when He calls you to that which will give you life; and know that Allah comes in between a man and his heart, and that it is He to Whom you shall (all) be gathered."[16]

However, some of Islam's laws appear more vigorous than others, for example:

A. The law of *"Bayt_el_Maal"[17]*

B. The law of *"The dominion of people over their wealth and selves"*

C. The law of *"Whoever precedes others to something not claimed by another Muslim, has more right to it."[18]*

D. The law of *"The land belongs to Allah and to whoever develops it."[19]*

It is important for the young Islamic government to pay great attention and devotion to these laws and plan to earnestly and realistically implement these laws.

---

[16] The holy Qur'an: Public Estate [8]: 24.

[17] This may be referred to as the Central Bank or the Treasury.

[18] To use an analogy this is similar to say 'first come first serve' basis.

[19] These principles, in parts B, C, D have been stated by the Messenger of Allah (S).

A. The law of *"Bayt_el_Maal"* meets the needs of the poor such that the nation will be content with this policy since the surplus (of wealth) is distributed amongst the entire nation.

B. The law of *"The dominion of people over their wealth and selves"* gives people vast freedoms, which would satisfy various groups of society and facilitates opportunities to exercise their rights and activities.

Naturally a human being does not agree to the dominion of others over himself and their intervention into his affairs. If he realises that the government provides the opportunity to freely conduct his affairs - except for the forbidden ones - then he would be satisfied with the regime and would co-operate with it and its rule.

This is why we see stability, continuation and prosperity of democratic governments whereas dictatorial governments fall quickly because they create poor and abject nation that cannot find a way to fulfil its needs.

C. The law of *" Precedence"* gives people the opportunity to use all of the earth's resources within the framework of *"for you"*[20]

D. The law of *"The land belongs to Allah and to whoever develops it"* in association with above law does not leave anyone able to work with any need.

> With the inclusion of the law of *Bayt_el_Maal* to this, there will be no individual unable to work with a need.

The west has implemented some of these laws and has consequently made significant progress, whereas Muslims abandoned these laws and the result was their painful decline and downfall, which is unprecedented in Islamic history. Imam Ali (A) (addressing the Muslims) said:

"By Allah! By Allah! Let not others precede you in practicing the teachings of the Qur'an."

Therefore it is imperative for the newly established Islamic government to abide earnestly to these and similar laws, which would

---

[20] "It is He Who has created **for you** all things that are on earth..." - The holy Qur'an: The Heifer [2]: 29.

please Allah and the *Ommah* (Islamic community) because such measures lead to prosperity and perfection.

It is also important to revive the principle of 'Muslim Brotherhood' that allows every Muslim (from any country) to engage in all activities in the Islamic State which the Muslims of the country concerned can participate in, such as land ownership, marriage, business, "*precedence*" to the permissible[21], etc.

For example, if an Islamic government were to be established in Iraq, and since Iraq is an important centre for Islamic universities and contains many holy shrines in its cities, anyone who wanted to visit the holy shrines or to study must be allowed to travel to and stay in Iraq, similar to the way it used to be since the beginning of Islam. A visitor and a student should have total freedom to do what they wish within the Islamic and humanitarian framework.

---

[21] The permissible is anything that is not forbidden or restricted in Islam. In Islam there are some restrictions on some aspects and beyond that, anything, which is not prohibited or restricted, is referred to as permissible.

The Penal System

Order and security are not established unless the guilty are chastised. Under Islamic jurisdiction the prescribed punishment are grouped in two categories:

1. For transgressing the right of Allah, e.g. consumption of alcohol or committing adultery.

2. For transgressing the right of an individual such as murder or defamation.

Under Islamic jurisdiction, both kinds of punishments have been prescribed, as mentioned in the book of *"The predefined-penalties and punishment"*.[22]

Although the Council of Jurists must be referred to and consulted with, but in my view if an Islamic government is established, all punishments in the above two categories must be deferred to disciplinary (measures) for five years, say.

This deferment could be in the form of disciplinary detention or something similar so as to serve as a deterrent - as deemed by the Council of Jurists as well as the experts in the field - who would determine the form and length of detention. This is to give the government a chance to establish itself and take control so as to allow Islam to be implemented from the points of view of aspects such as economy, society, politics, all of which are related to punishment. Here a number of issues are taken into consideration:

1. The Messenger of Allah, (S), did not implement the penal system until after implementing Islamic rule in the holy city of Medina and he, (S), is an example[23] (to us). The Messenger of

---

[22] M. Shirazi, *al-Fiqh* series, vols. 87-88.
[23] *"You have indeed in the Messenger of Allah a beautiful pattern (of conduct)"* - The holy Qur'an: The Confederates [33]: 21.

Allah (S) implemented the laws as a complete and indivisible system.

2. Allah the Almighty states in the noble Qur'an: ***"Do no mischief on the earth, after it has been reformed."***[24] Therefore, before the complete and total implementation of Islam, there can be no reform!

3. The principle of "Priorities", which is a principle based on reason and rationale and is referred to in the noble Qur'an:

> *"And were it not that mankind might become of one (evil) way of life, We would provide, for everyone that blasphemes against the Most Gracious (Allah), silver roofs for their houses, and (silver) stair-ways on which to go up, . . ."*[25]

(When one wishes to implement a law or a principle but is confronted with another issue which causes conflict, then, given the priorities of the circumstances one may have to revise the plan or even decide to abandon the plan altogether in order to prevent greater difficulties as can be seen from above Qur'anic verse. A number of other precedents may be cited, such as:)

The Messenger of Allah (S) on a number of occasions had stated that

"Were it not for the people to say . . ."

(This means the Messenger of Allah (S) would have carried out his intended plan were it not for another issue which conflicted with his plan and therefore he, (S), judged that the outcome of his intended plan would be in conflict with the other issue, hence did not proceed with his plan(s).)

The Messenger of Allah (S) is quoted as saying

"Were it not for your people being recent converts to Islam, I would have demolished the Ka'bah and rebuilt it with two doors."

Imam Ali (A) is quoted as saying:

" . . . one battalion of my army would have been demolished."

---

[24] The holy Qur'an: The Ramparts [7]: 56.
[25] The holy Qur'an: Adornment [43]: 33.

21

Imam Ali (A) ignored those who performed a new kind of prayer despite the fact the Messenger of Allah, (S), banned it but they remained undeterred.

The Messenger of Allah (S) did not punish those who deserted the battle as well as those who had committed various sins.

This is so that Islam is not misunderstood and its reputation not tarnished, amongst other reasons. (The teaching of Islam regarding punishment of the guilty may only be carried out if, and only if, all of the preconditions and criteria of the individual concerned and the circumstances are totally met. Otherwise the conviction will be null and void and the punishment, if executed, will constitute a sin and be against the teaching of Islam. Furthermore this will give the wrong impression of Islam, detrimental to its pure and true message. As a result, others (Muslims and non-Muslims alike) would conclude that the teaching of Islam is harsh, inhumane and incorrect and therefore Islam is incapable of addressing the issues of human affairs.)

Therefore predefined-penalties (*Hodud*) may not be executed in enemy land as we discussed, in details, in book series *al-Fiqh*, "*Jurisprudence Fundamentals*"[26].

Furthermore we have the principle that *"The predefined-penalties are waived by doubt"* and that Islam has laid down comprehensive set of preconditions and criteria (which must be met before any punishment is executed) to the extent that some of them prove to be sometimes inhibitory.

This is because Islam uproots corruption, so that there will be no poverty, . . . and natural crimes will significantly reduce. The course of Islamic history is a testimony to this fact.

The vast number of problems and high levels of corruption in Muslim countries that we see today is due to abandoning Islamic laws, suppressing people's freedoms, widespread injustice, tyranny, etc.

The penal system, therefore, may not be implemented unless other Islamic laws are implemented so that a government provides all the necessities of complete and healthy life for the people.

---

[26] M. Shirazi, al-Fiqh series, vol. 141.

Possession of Real Power

It is imperative that a multi-party, consultative regime must enjoy an adequate level of deterrent power. This is important since the existence of power would deter and apprehend the enemies especially those who consider the establishment of a consultative system a danger to them. The benefit of such power would foil their attempts to topple the young system of government. Furthermore, the presence of an adequate power would stabilise the security (of the state) and give confidence to people. Hence, a regime that does not possess an adequate deterrent force will not be able to establish itself and, if it did manage to do so, it would not be able to survive.

The provision of power is that there be fundamental constituents of proper organisation and discipline as well as political, military and economic power; and strong management procedure to enable the young regime to survive the onslaught of enemies and opportunists.

We note that the Messenger of Allah (S) in Medina, where people used to *"enter Allah's Religion in throngs"*[27] was the same messenger (S) who lived in Makkah. Allah the Almighty outlines the state of His Messenger, (S), when he was in Makkah in early times of his mission as: *"Remember how the Unbelievers plotted against you, to keep you in bonds, or slay you, or get you out (of your home)."*[28] And in another occasion Allah states:

"... when the Unbelievers drove him out ..."[29]

In both locations (Makkah and Medina), the Messenger of Allah (S) was the same person; the conveyor of the divine revelation and the guide to the right path, all the time and everywhere he always was pure, sacrosanct, infallible, at the peak of virtue and excellence and

---

[27] The holy Qur'an: The Support [110]: 2.
[28] The holy Qur'an: Public Estate [8]: 30.
[29] The holy Qur'an: Repentance [9]: 40.

supported by the divine sanction. However, the difference was in power. In Makkah, the Islamic mission was in its infancy and it did not have the necessary power to confront the pagans directly and therefore the Messenger of Allah (S) suffered extreme torment at the pagans' hands.

In Medina, on the other hand, the Messenger of Allah (S) gained sufficient power such that it was the manifestation of Allah's statement: *" And make ready for them whatever you can of power and horses to terrify thereby the enemies of Allah and your enemies. "[30]* It was then that he attained such a high worldly status.

Power may be classified into two categories:

1.   Power of the Despots,

2.   Power of the Consultative.

There is a vast contrast between the two. The consultative power is a power of tranquillity, which is likely to survive. It does not turn into a means of destroying the nation and consuming its resources. The despotic power, on the other hand, lives on for a limited period during which it is stained by vices, murders, persecution and terrorism. Everyone observed the destruction of the likes of the communist Soviet Union, Eastern Germany, Enver Hoxha of Albania, Ceausescu of Romania, and Kim Il Sung and other similar despots. Despotism drove those countries to breakdown, which destroyed the infrastructures of those countries and annihilated their resources.

Therefore it is imperative that those in the Islamic movement gain an honest and righteous power of the consultative kind, which is based on freedom, free elections, and system of multi-party pluralism.

As for the despotic power, in effect it lacks the real power since the power that is based on despotism is a fallacious power subject to quick collapse: *" . . .for Allah is swift in account. "[31]* and if some considered it to be long term then: *"They see it as distant, but We see it close"[32]*

---

[30] The holy Qur'an: Public Estate [8]: 60.
[31] The holy Qur'an: The Family of 'Emran [3]: 199.
[32] The holy Qur'an: The Ways of Ascent [70]: 6-7.

24

10

Distribution of Power

Competition is a natural phenomenon, which has coexisted with mankind throughout history. Even for heaven there is competition for good deeds as Allah has stated:

"... Over that, let the competitors compete"[33] and

"And hasten to forgiveness from your Lord"[34] and

"So strive, as in a race, in all virtues."[35]

As for this world, competition results in mankind's vitality and sharpens his resolve more and more to the extent that he tries to outpace others. He makes sure that he does not fall behind other competitors through innovation and development. As a result, his scientific and practical achievements will be reflected on society, which subsequently lead to his progress and success.

Therefore it is important for the newly established government to create a state of healthy and positive competition of free political parties that are firmly rooted in society and are based on constitutional establishments. This will create an incentive towards progress and everyone will play his/her role to the best of their abilities in the various fields of labour and expertise.

We see this clearly in the life of the Messenger of Allah (S). The Messenger of Allah (S) classified the Muslims into two factions, the Migrants and the Supporters and incited competition between them. The criterion of an individual's capability and competence was his/her ability to do a good deed well. This was despite the fact that the Messenger of Allah (S) treated people equally in the domains of doctrine, worship, transactions, human rights and status before the

---

[33] The Qur'an: Fraudsters [83]: 26.
[34] The Qur'an: Family of 'Emraan [3]: 133.
[35] The Qur'an: Table Spread [5]: 48.

law, since equality is a basic principle in Islam, as stated by Allah the Almighty:

"O mankind! We created you from a single (pair) of a male and a female, and made you into nations and tribes, so that you may come to know each other. Verily the most honoured of you in the sight of Allah is the most righteous of you."[36] And also

"Surely the believers are brothers."[37] And it has been reported, *"Truly the people are from Adam and Adam is from dust."*

On this basis, it is suggested that the origin of the 'political parties' in the name Hizb (Arabic for political parties) existed at the era of the Messenger of Allah (S), be it in its primitive form. The Messenger of Allah (S) is reported as saying "I am in the party in which Ibn al-Adra' is."

Therefore, any group that wants to form a party should be free to do so. The number of parties may not be limited, but the party activity must not contradict Islam because the population in Muslim countries are predominantly Muslims.

National parties are acceptable because such parties intend to develop the Muslim countries in the various political, social, and economical fields.

---

[36] The holy Qur'an: The Chambers [49]: 13.
[37] The holy Qur'an: The Chambers [49]: 10.

11

Freedoms

Freedom is a fundamental principle which gives right to an individual to choose from, say or do or . . . anything according to the individual's wishes, as established by reason and Islamic jurisprudence.

It is therefore the responsibility of the newly established Islamic government to grant freedom in all dominions to the people - within the framework of Islam. Freedom encompasses all aspects such as those in belief, expression, agriculture, business, trade, manufacture, employment, travel, residency, construction, procurement of the permissible, setting up radio and television stations, printing, establishing political parties, publishing newspapers and magazines, etc. We have detailed these in the book of *Freedoms* in the *al-Fiqh* series.[38]

Thus all kinds of restrictions and repressions are annulled; such as ID cards, nationality documents, passports, licence to import/export, etc.

In brief, everyone is free in everything except that which is unlawful, which are very few indeed. Furthermore, what is unlawful for the Muslims may not be so for the non-Muslims, in accordance with the *'Binding'*[39] principle as discussed in length in the book of *"Jurisprudence Fundamentals"* of the *al-Fiqh* series[40].

The Messenger of Allah, Muhammad (S) *said "whoever embraced the religion of a people then he is subject to their laws."*

History shows us that people who embraced Islam or those who chose to live in Islamic countries under Islamic law did so because of

---

[38] M. Shirazi, *al-Fiqh* series, vol. 139, *"Freedoms"*.

[39] This principle is based on the teaching of the Messenger of Allah (S) when said regarding the doctrinal and judicial treatment of the non-Muslims, *"Enjoin on them whatever they have enjoined on themselves".*

[40] M. Shirazi, *al-Fiqh* series, vol. 141, *"Jurisprudence Fundamentals"*.

the vast and widespread freedoms practised under that system, whereas there were no such provisions in any other part of the world under any religion, jurisdiction, or government. This was in a way similar to governments of the so-called free world today. Although it is a free world relative to other countries of the world, it is not so with respect to the correct Islamic system of government.

Some might think that this would bring about chaos and anarchy. The answer to that is that freedom has never been associated with chaos over the thirteen centuries of Islamic history. But when Muslim countries adopted the rule of western laws, Muslims became trapped in untold sufferings, tragedies and problems. I myself observed great number of Islamic freedoms in Iraq half a century ago, which we subsequently lost after the Second World War.[41] I referred to some of those freedoms in the book *"Remnants of Islamic Civilisation as I saw them"*[42]

As for the chaos and disturbance we see in our countries today, it is due to dictatorship and despotism. Despotism is a plague-full swamp, which infects the society with diseases such as tyranny, oppression, poverty, persecution, imprisonment, expulsion, wars, etc.

---

[41] After WW II, the British forces occupied Iraq, and as a result of their control and influence, western laws and regulations replaced the Islamic laws that were in that country.
[42] See also *"Our lives Half a Century Ago"*, by the author.

12

Security

At this day and age, the security service is a cornerstone of the government in order to counter the attempts of opponents who aim to penetrate the government, either to bring about its downfall or to derail it from its Islamic and humanitarian course.

A security service must be set-up to counter the external enemy whose aim is to destroy the regime elected by people. It must not be used to confront the nation, just as tyrant rulers in despotic regimes use the security service to oppress the nation, suppressing the talents and potentials of its people and glorifying the tyrant as a 'great leader'.

According to Islamic jurisprudence and rationale, spying is forbidden except on the officials of the government and its agencies, starting from the head of state. This is in order to ensure that they are not diverted (from their duties) and that they do not neglect or disregard the interest of the nation. Spying is also allowed on offensive enemies who are actively engaged in attempts to destabilise the order and security of the country - like the international security agencies today.

A correct security system, which serves the interest of the nation, does so within a consultative system that relies on and is supported by free political parties, free elections and constitutional establishments. It is only then that the security organ becomes pivotal to the survival of the government, to its power, progress and becomes the guardian of the nation's interests and resources.

It is therefore important that the nation monitors the performance and activity of this organ and holds it accountable in accordance with the Islamic principle of *"Enjoin Good and Forbid Evil"*. This is to ensure that the security organ does not have a free hand in doing whatever they like to do, and that it does not misuse their authority and go beyond their prescribed function. Also, the organ must be strong and competent enough to meet the challenges of the day, given the great technological and cultural progress.

In order to ensure that the security agency becomes the guardian of the nation's interests, besides monitoring the service and its competence, it is necessary to strengthen and focus its faith in Allah and the hereafter and its fear of the Almighty overtly and covertly. This is of course required for every one of the agencies of the Islamic system of government. Only then will the security service be able to discharge its duties truthfully and precisely, which would subsequently lead to strengthening the regime. Thus, the Islamic country will become representative of a regime of correctness and dexterity.

A reported Tradition states:

"May Allah have mercy upon he who performs a task and perfects it." Another states:

" . . . but Allah loves one who, when performing a task, performs excellently."

As for what is found today under despotic regimes in terms of spying on and monitoring the nation, depriving its freedoms and harming it, those are amongst the most forbidden; Allah the Almighty states: *"Do not spy"*[43].

---

[43] The holy Qur'an: the Chambers [49]: 12.

13

Valuing Professionals

The prophet Joseph said: ***"I am a good guardian and expert"***[44].

Professional and technical jobs require reliability for which Joseph said ***"good guardian"*** as well as expertise for which he said, ***"good expert"***.

Therefore it is important that the young Islamic government pays good attention to experts and professionals in every field of the government. Loyalty towards the government should not be the only criterion in appointing staff to a position. Such policies would cause complications and difficulties. Should this happen, the management of the government would be in unqualified and incompetent hands, which would subsequently result in many mistakes and errors. The presence of government loyalists within its agencies must be balanced with the provision of necessary expertise in order to safeguard the country and its progress. The presence of one group without the other would result in the state of the country resembling that of a bird with one wing.

We have witnessed the destruction caused as a result of such policies in countries governed by revolutionaries after military *coup d'état*. The state of destruction was such that people of the country wished the previous government back. A poet pictures this state of affair in his poem as:

Would the oppression of Sons of Marwan[45] ***come back to us***

And would the justice of Sons of Abbas[46] ***never was***

---

[44] The holy Qur'an: Joseph [12]: 55.

[45] Refers to a tyrant dynasty that began its bloodthirsty rule of the Islamic State in 685, i.e. 55 years after the death of the Messenger of Allah Muhammad (S).

31

In such cases revolutionaries and government loyalists cause more difficulties by confiscation, imprisonment, executions and making empty promises - all in a bid to strengthen their positions of power and force people to accept that they are the best. This way, they enter into confrontation with the people, subsequently leading to their own downfall.

It is possible to address the problem of reliability and expertise by pairing one with the other. Although this could prove difficult, the difficulty of giving the helm to anyone of them is even greater, and will have a worse consequence.

Clearly, this is not possible in a despotic regime in which power is centralised because unquestioned power corrupts and gets corrupted.

---

[46] Refers to the Abbasid dynasty that toppled the Marwan dynasty around 705.

14

Minorities and Political Parties

The Islamic government coexists with minorities peacefully. Minorities have rules and laws specific to them, whether they are religious minorities such as Jews and Christians, or non-religious minorities such as Buddhists and Brahmans etc. Just as the Messenger of Allah (S) treated the pagans of Makkah, where he (S) did not force anyone of them to Islam after the fall of Makkah.

As far as the judiciary is concerned, minorities have the choice of referring to us or to their respective judiciary and judges. If they refer to us, we shall issue judgements for or against them according to their jurisdiction or ours.[47]

For general conducts such as traffic regulations, they must follow the law of the land, as is the case for every country in the world.

They pay the *Jizyah*[48] tax in exchange for the protection they receive from the Islamic head of state for their lives, wealth and family, just as Muslims pay the *Khums*[49] and *Zakat*[50] taxes. In contracts such as

---

[47] For more details see the *al-Fiqh* series, vols. 84-85; "The Judiciary", vol. 140; "The Law", vol. 141; "Jurisprudence Fundamentals" by the author.

[48] This is the tax that is paid by the non-Muslims under the Islamic system. The non-Muslims do not pay either the *Khums* or the *Zakat* taxes. They are not obliged to join the armed forces to defend the Islamic State whereas the Muslims are. The defence of the non-Muslims' lives, wealth, dignity etc. is the responsibility of the Islamic State. See M. Shirazi, *al-Fiqh* series, vol. 108, "Economics"; pp 41-42.

[49] Tax of 20% levied on untaxed, superfluous annual income. The taxed capital is not subjected to future *Khums* tax. Details in M. Shirazi, *al-Fiqh* series, vol. 33, "*Khums*".

[50] Tax on nine items when over certain limit. These items are Wheat, Barley, Dates, Raisins, Gold, Silver, Camels, Cows, and Sheep. Details in M. Shirazi, *al-Fiqh* series, vols. 29-32, "*Zakat*".

Kheraaj[51] and *Moqasemah*[52], there is no differential treatment between Muslims and non-Muslims.

Other laws of the country that must be respected are those such as: not to engage in forbidden practices in public like consuming alcohol in public, setting up brothels, etc. Details of these are discussed in the book of "*Islamic Government*" of the *al-Fiqh* series[53].

Non-Islamic, but nationalist political parties which aim to develop and prosper the country are allowed to function, and so too are minorities political parties which aim to function within their own particular sphere. However, political parties that call for activities opposing Islam are not allowed to operate.

Every political party is allowed to pursue its activities within the framework of Islam, regardless of its nationality or sect it belongs to. Every ethnic group may use their particular language in schools, newspapers, and mass media.

Needless to say, the official international language for Muslims is the Arabic language, since it is the language of the holy Qur'an and the sacred Sunnah. However, it is the right of any language speaking ethnic group to import radio and television station and printing presses and to publish newspapers and magazines in their own language.

---

[51] This is the income from letting a particular category of land. Details in M. Shirazi, *al-Fiqh* series, vols. 107-108, "*Economics*".

[52] This is a kind of a contract where the profits are divided based on the original investment or number of shares.

[53] M. Shirazi, *al-Fiqh* series, vols. 101-102, "*The Islamic Government*".

15

International Relations

The countries of the world are categorised into two groups in relation to the Islamic State, which will be established by the will of Allah:

1. Islamic countries,

2. Non-Islamic countries.

As for Islamic countries, it must be dealt with in accordance with Islamic jurisdiction on the basis of one community, Islamic brotherhood and Islamic freedom. Allah the Almighty states:

"And verily this community of yours is a single community, and I am your Lord therefore fear Me."[54]

"Surely the believers are brothers."[55]

"He releases them from their heavy burdens and from the yokes that are upon them."[56]

Therefore, a Muslim from any other country must be treated equally like any other Muslim citizen of the Islamic State. Unless there was a definite *"Secondary Order"*[57] such as the laws of the *"No Harm"*, *"Priorities"* and *"Precedence"* where the forerunner takes precedence over others. However, the *"Secondary Order"* is applied only in exceptional circumstances and not as a fundamental principle. It is also on a temporary basis only, and not a permanent one.

I recall about half a century ago, when there were no concepts such as ID cards and nationality or citizenship documents and suchlike, Muslims from other countries, Islamic or non-Islamic, used to come to Iraq. They were accorded the same status as those of Muslims in

---

[54] The holy Qur'an: the Believers [23]: 52.
[55] The holy Qur'an: the Chambers [49]: 10.
[56] The holy Qur'an: the Ramparts [7]: 157.
[57] In his other works the author has explained that the "Secondary Orders" are defined by deputies in consultation with the Council of Jurists.

Iraq in every respect such as marriage, business, employment, fraternity, etc. This status quo must be revived in accordance with Allah's order in the glorious book.

A non-Muslim who comes to the Islamic state will be treated according to the *'Binding'* law[58], the *'Exchange of Interests'* and ***"Allah forbids you not, with regard to those who fight you not for (your) Faith nor drive you out of your homes, from dealing kindly and justly with them: for Allah loves those who are just."***[59]

This is in addition to the aforementioned exceptional laws such as the *"No Harm"* and *"Priorities"* principles.

Some Muslim and non-Muslim countries might wage war against the young Islamic State. This may be due to conflicting interests, or due to traditional animosities or other factors such as enemy designs and conspiracies etc. In all these cases, the problem must be resolved by the best possible means. This is the merit that distinguishes a wise government from an immature one. In fact, just as arrogant and selfishness destroys individuals, they destroy governments too. The scale of destruction of a government is faster and more widespread, as the saying goes *"If a scholar gets corrupt, the world would follow"* and *"A corrupt scholar would corrupt the world"*.

Therefore it is imperative that animosity must change to co-operation at least to a certain extent. If, in the worst-case scenario, it was not possible (to change animosity to co-operation), and this is a rare assumption, then it is important to adopt a position of, at least, non-animosity to avoid a problem.

---

[58] This principle is based on the teaching of the Messenger of Allah (S) when said regarding the doctrinal and judicial treatment of the non-Muslims, *"Enjoin on them whatever they have enjoined on themselves"*.
[59] The holy Qur'an: the Tested [60]: 8.

16

Good Neighbourliness

One of the most important ingredients of stability for the young Islamic state is good neighbourliness, and respect for the right of the neighbour not just in a good way but in the best possible way, as Allah the Almighty states:

"And enjoin your people to hold fast by the best in the precepts."[60]

Imam Kaadhum (A) is reported as saying:

"Good neighbourliness is not abstaining from harming (the neighbour), but good neighbourliness is to persevere with the harm (coming from the neighbour)."

If a neighbour was a bad one in terms of belief or behaviour, it is imperative to reform him and invite him (to good) in the best possible way as Allah the Almighty states in the noble Qur'an:

"Invite (all) to the Way of thy Lord with wisdom and beautiful preaching; and argue with them in ways that are best and most gracious."[61]

If good neighbourliness is important in relation to neighbouring houses in small communities, it is more so with respect to countries and governments.

The Islamic government must ensure that all its dealings are based on wisdom and reason with all countries - whether geographically close such as neighbour countries or distant ones such as all other countries of the world, Muslim and non-Muslim countries alike.

If an opposing country starts a media campaign of agitation against the young Islamic state, it is important that the Islamic state keeps its nerves with all its resolve. It should respond to the insult with

---

[60] The holy Qur'an: the Ramparts [7]: 145.
[61] The holy Qur'an: the Bee [16]: 125.

kindness and reply *"with wisdom and beautiful preaching"*[62], not with insult and ridicule. The outcome of that kindness is at least to lessen the insult.

Imam Sajjad (A) said:

"O lord have Mercy on Muhammad and his descendants . . . and help me to tender with sincerity whoever cheated me, and to reward with kindness whoever abandoned me, and to repay generously whoever denied me, and to recompense by making bond with whoever broke off with me, and to praise whoever backbite against me. Enable me to appreciate the good deed and forgive the bad deed."[63]

Accordingly, the Noble Qur'an states: *"To forgo is nearest to righteousness"*[64]

The Messiah Jesus (A) is reported to have said: *"If someone slaps your right cheek turn your left cheek for him."* Here he wanted the honour and comfort of the person being slapped before that of the slapping individual, because tolerating one slap is easier than putting up with many which will happen in case a fight erupts between the two. But this calls for strong nerves and use of reason and deliberation.

Naturally, in any case, the circumstances and priorities must be considered in line with the recommendations of the council of jurists.

---

[62] ibid.

[63] Extracts from supplications of Imam Sajjad (A) known as *"Makaarem al-Akhlaaq"* or "The Noble Ethics".

[64] The holy Qur'an, the Heifer [2]: 237.

Economic Development

Economy is one of the most important aspects which the young Islamic government must pay attention to, since *"He who does not have a sustenance, does not have the hereafter"*[65] as reported in the sacred Tradition of the Messenger of Allah (S). The Messenger of Allah (S) is also quoted as saying: *"Poverty is a shame in both worlds".*

Economic independence brings about political independence, whereas inflation, high prices, and scarcity of income cause disaffection of the government, which subsequently results in its downfall. The way forward in order to secure a healthy and developing economy is to execute an accurate program for the overall economy.

The government must create - and allow others to do so - economic institutions and think tanks of experts in various sectors of the economy, such as agriculture, manufacture, trade, import and export, banking system, etc. The government must ensure that laws related to the economy are modern, dynamic and in accordance with Islamic jurisprudence. All of this is within the framework of "free capital" in the true sense of the word - and legitimate - *"You shall have your capital"*[66].

---

[65] One who does not earn the means of his sustenance does not have an honourable life and therefore he may have to ask for handouts from others, which is a disgrace, or may be forced to steal or cheat to make ends meet, which is an even worse behaviour. Whereas the individual who has a source of income can lead a decent life and have an honourable family which is the nucleus of society and the Almighty desired for mankind in this world, for which He will reward in the hereafter.

[66] The holy Qur'an, the Heifer [2]: 279. The complete verse reads as follows: *"If you do it not (give up usury), take notice of war from Allah and His Messenger: but if you turn back, you shall have your capital sums; neither you shall make (anyone) suffer nor shall you be made to suffer."*

All affairs are in the hands of people. The government's role is that of the regulator only. This is true also for airports, railways, industries - large and small - hospitals, etc. Freedom should be for all people to make use of land, since *"land belongs to Allah and to whoever revitalises it"*. Water, forests and procurement of the permissible such as fishes and other animals, the various minerals in accordance with the law of the *"Precedence"*, should be in the hands of people. As Allah the Almighty has stated: *"for you"*[67]. All of this is only achievable within the framework of the primary Islamic laws and the secondary laws such as the laws of *"no harm"* and *"priorities"* in accordance with their jurisprudence criteria as described by religious authorities and on the basis of the consultation with the 'Council of Jurists' and the 'house of representatives' and the 'committees of experts'.

As for what is practised today, like banning people from procuring the permissible and denying them their economic freedoms, it is illegal according to Islamic jurisprudence, and it is one of the greatest dangers to the stability, prosperity and progress of any Islamic government.

Some of the important cornerstones of economic development are "self-sufficiency", "reduction of civil servants to absolute minimum", "free political parties", "industrialising the country ","mass education and awareness".

In this manner, poverty and unemployment will be eradicated, and everybody will be able to obtain their primary and secondary requirements.

One of the most important aspects of a healthy economy is to have free business and free manufacturing sectors in the full meaning of the word, except in the forbidden dealings, which are very few indeed.

Given the importance of the economy - rationally and in accordance with Islamic teaching - it would reflect positively on the stature of the government and, in turn, lead to broad international horizons. Therefore if the young government achieves a healthy economy, it

---

[67] The holy Qur'an, the Heifer [2]: 29, "*It is He Who has created for you all things that are on earth; then He turned to the heaven and made them into seven firmaments. And of all things He has perfect knowledge.*"

will set a good standard for others to follow. This is of course good for the prosperity of the people in this world and the hereafter.

The non-Muslims adopted the policies of Muslims in science, freedom, technology, etc. even though they lived during the dark Middle Ages, at a time when Muslims were going through cultural and scientific renaissance. As a result, non-Muslims progressed formidably while Muslims abandoned their own advancements and remained underdeveloped and backward.

18

Self-sufficiency

Amir_ol_Mu'meneen, Ali (A), has said, *"Become needy to anyone you wish and you will become his captive"*. It is obvious that anyone who needs another person will become dependent upon him and subordinate to him. One will lead in any way he wishes and if the other refuses to follow, he will be denied his handout.

The west did not overwhelm and dominate other countries through military force only, but also through financial handouts to the third world countries and supplying them with experts, etc.

For this reason, the Messenger of Allah (S), after arriving in the city of Medina, which in effect became the capital city for Muslims, gave high priority to self-sufficiency of Muslims so that they would not be subjected to domination of the Jews of Medina.

In a well-known event, the caliph of the time wanted to give some money to *Abu Tharr*, may the blessings of Allah be upon him, but he refused to accept it. The caliph's envoy to *Abu Tharr* - who was the caliph's slave and was promised his freedom if he manages to give the money to *Abu Tharr* - said to *Abu Tharr*: "if you take this money I shall win my freedom". *Abu Tharr* replied "but I shall lose mine".

A newly established Islamic government must give high priority to self-sufficiency in various aspects of life ranging from food, drink and housing to agriculture, manufacture, banking, etc.

This may be addressed through commissioning various high-ranking committees of experts and professionals and taking a number of steps:

1. The use of agricultural lands and developing animal resources such as poultry and fish farming etc. and other manufacturing and production activities,

2. The young Islamic government must concern itself with industrialising the country through the creation of factories and

manufacturing plants, which in turn would employ substantial number of workers, the consequent of which is progress towards independence and self-sufficiency.

Industrialisation must include small local industries as well as large national ones. For example in Iraq towards the end of the monarchy rule - when there was a degree of pluralism and free political parties and some stability - there were some 400 products being manufactured in the holy city of Karbala.

Furthermore, industrial development is one of the most important factors, which contribute to the progress of a nation in all different fields, because manufacturing ability ranks highest amongst all the cultural, educational, expertise and social fields.

Industry facilitates the provision of the country's needs, brings about self-sufficiency, reduces unemployment to a minimum, eliminates poverty and destitution and prevents inflation. All of these in turn play their respective roles in reducing immorality, theft, illness, drug abuse and other similar vices.

Needless to say, industrial development and progress is only achieved with the existence of freedom, pluralism, minimum staffing level, absence of bureaucracy, investment and incentive for investment, etc. Also, people must be encouraged to create investment and loan trusts, as well as, Mudahrabah (investment) banks, which would take part in the industrialisation process and development.

We have previously mentioned that freedom may not exist unless it is supported by free political parties and constitutional institutions.

Therefore if the government concerned itself with this matter and started to gradually build the industrial sector, first through setting up small factories and then, according to circumstances and available resources, address the issues of heavy industries, in five years the country would be on the verge of self-sufficiency in the fields of manufacture and agriculture. This will subsequently lead to self - sufficiency in other fields.[68]

---

[68] The author presents more discussions on this topic in *"The Means to Muslim Renaissance"*, *"The Criteria of Victory"*, al-Fiqh series, vols. 107-108, *"Economics"*.

It can be seen that some of the third world countries spend most of their expenditure on consumption and completely rely on importing their consumables from abroad to meet their fundamental and luxury needs. Therefore they become dependant on and captive of the countries they rely on. The situation is exacerbated when they borrow from those (exporting) countries to pay for their imports. However, if they used the resources to strengthen their economic structure and ability, they would achieve self-sufficiency.

19

Combating Unemployment

One of the causes that contribute to the spread of social vices is unemployment, which leads the society towards destruction and disintegration. Unemployment drags the unemployed to moral deprivation, theft, crime, disease, suicide, ignorance, anarchy, etc. One who does not have a job sells his body to earn money, or steals for that purpose or engages in various crimes and even infidelity, the Messenger of Allah (S) is reported as saying *"Poverty leads to infidelity"*. He is also quoted as saying, *"Poverty is the shame of both worlds"*.

Abu Tharr is quoted as saying *"It surprises me how the poor do not rise against the rich with their swords!"*

An example of the aspect which surprised Abu Tharr has been manifested recently when Communism - which is the pit of poverty and corruption - came into existence but people did not tolerate the humility of captivity, poverty and repression (associated with Communism) for longer than a short period, compared to the lives of major countries and civilisations. The people relieved themselves from that misery and brought down the Communist regime.

A destitute person who is unemployed may develop a psychological complex, which would reflect on the health of the individual since body and soul affect one another.

Furthermore, in many cases, poverty and unemployment directly cause diseases and illnesses such as lack of ability and means of receiving medical treatment, stomach ulcer, stroke, anaemia and all consequences of stress and nervous breakdown. That is why we read in our supplication: *"O' Allah enrich every poor and destitute (person)."*

Also, a poor and destitute person does not have the means to finance his education and therefore his situation is exacerbated by ignorance even further. This subsequently gives him the potential to move towards instigation of anarchy, uprisings, wars, etc.

This is the cause in majority of cases, although unemployment may not always be associated with poverty and destitution, but we are talking about the majority of cases.

Therefore it is imperative upon the young Islamic government to plan effective solutions to eradicate unemployment. This could be through measure such as: giving freedoms, permissibility of ownership and revitalisation of land and all that Allah has created for the benefit of mankind - those which are not already owned by others - on the basis of the law of "*Precedence*" within the framework of *"for you"*. Job opportunities could also be created through encouraging the wealthy to invest in the production sector in order to create employment for those without jobs and other similar measures.

If some people still remained without jobs - after all those measures - they must have the provision to lead an honourable average life until they find a suitable job. This may be through the support and facilities of the *Bayt_el_Maal* and the encouragement of philanthropists to take part in this cause to eradicate deprivation. For this Allah states *"And would not encourage the feeding of the indigent!"*[69] And He has made this to be one of the causes of ending up in the hellfire.

---

[69] The holy Qur'an, The Certain Hour [69]: 34.

20

Civil Service Reform

It can be argued that the swelling of the civil service is worse than inflation of the economy or it can be one of its causes. This is because the inflation of the body of the civil service turns the producers into consumers and leads to domination of bureaucracy that limits people's freedoms. In this way the country heads towards deprivation and poverty after the ruling system takes over the wealth (of the nation) and denies its people the freedom of work and production.

Every surplus civil servant becomes a burden to the people and a barrier to their freedoms.

The role of the civil service is to secure the safety and security of the people as well as their welfare and to guard their interests. The size of the civil service that would accomplish such tasks adequately and at the same time not be a burden on the people nor a barrier to their freedoms is a size just adequate to manage the affairs of the government and serve its people. The civil service is there to serve the people and the civil servant has a role similar to that of a teacher or a driver or a pilot who the society needs.

However, to regard the civil service as a career would not serve the nation, nor it would protect its interest. It would become a job opportunity and a source of income, as is the case in many countries ruled by dictatorship. In those countries the civil service is the great calamity, since the civil service changes into a bureaucracy, which lays down laws that hinder the people's affairs and repress their freedoms. In such a case, the masses are transformed into subordinates to the civil servants instead of the other way round.

The swelling of the civil service is clearly noticeable in democratic countries too. This is because they have distanced themselves from the teachings of the prophets, peace be upon them (pbut). Those countries legislated many laws, which are in fact harmful to the society from many points of view.

As for dictatorial regimes, the expansion is far greater. It is therefore imperative for the newly established Islamic government to commission working groups to eradicate surplus civil servants and transfer them to the productive sector.

As for members of staff that are removed from the service - because of being surplus to requirement since their role had changed to consumption (of salaries) and repression of freedoms - they must be transferred to a productive sector. The government must assist them to become productive elements in the economy or other profession so that they do not face poverty and unemployment. This may be accomplished through detailed studies carried out by experts who would base their correct criteria in accordance with rationale and Islamic jurisdiction.

In my view, if a government seriously and honestly addresses this issue, there will be none of this massive body of the civil service except for less than 10% of its current size, which is sufficient for the government to run the affair of the country. We have presented a detailed discussion about this matter in some of the works related to aspects of "*Government in Islam*"[70].

---

[70] M. Shirazi, *al-Fiqh* series, vol. 99. See also:
"The Islamic Government during the Reign of Amir_ol_Mu'meneen",
"The Government of the Messenger of Allah (S) and Amir_ol_Mu'meneen",
"The Islamic System of Government" by the author.

21

Simplicity and Provision of Fundamental

Necessities

The implementation of the policy of simplicity in various aspects of life brings about bliss as well as mental and physical comfort. In contrast, complicated life styles give an individual nothing but disease and illness, even though this kind of life style carries with it material beauty, grandeur and vanity.

For this reason, Islam insists strongly on simplicity in all affairs; personal, social, through to national and governmental.

For example, a judge takes up a position in a mosque and uses the mosque as his site to make his judgement where people can clearly see and hear him. People can look at the details of his judgements and his dealings without any cover or division, or any guards, pomp, ceremony or any delay in the judgement or its execution and without any fees or charges. These will give the people total assurance to the validity of his judgement. People are also assured that it is not possible for the judge to deprive their rights nor is it possible for him to favour one group over another. Similarly simplicity should be adopted in other aspects of life, such as birth, marriage, death, hospitality, travel, house, shop, and a thousand and one other things.

For example the Messenger of Allah (S) said: *"The best of my nation's women are (those who have the) least dowry"*.

The Messenger of Allah (S) has also been quoted as saying: *"those people are blessed whose best utensils are clay"*.

The Messenger of Allah (S) also said: *"Make things easy, not difficult"*.

The noble Qur'an states: *"Allah intends every facility for you; He does not want to put you to difficulties."*[71] And the list goes on for hundreds of Qur'anic verses, traditions as well as policies adopted by the Messenger of Allah and his infallible progeny, *Ahl_ul_Bayt*, peace be upon them all.

Therefore it is incumbent upon an upcoming Islamic government to use simplicity in its system of government to the utmost degree possible and to educate the people upon that policy too.

If the ruling system uses simplicity in its affairs and conducts, then the people would follow suit, just as the saying goes: *"People follow the religion (way) of their kings."*

Furthermore, simplicity reduces ignorance, disease, poverty and various other problems, because complexity transforms life into an unnatural system, which upsets the balance of its health and social vitality.

---

[71] The holy Qur'an, the Heifer [2]: 185.

22

Modesty of Leaders

It is incumbent upon the leaders in Muslim countries and especially upon those of an Islamic government who want to implement the teachings of Islam to adhere to the principle of modesty and abstention from worldly vanities and be content with essential basic needs of life.

People are attracted by those who abstain from worldly vanities and comply with their commands. Through their modesty people realise the honesty of their leaders. As a result their places will be in the people's hearts . . . In one of the Salutations to Imam Hussain (A) he is addressed: *"your grave is in the heart of whoever loves you."* So all the splendour surrounding the caliphs collapsed and Imam Hussain (A) remained shining as a star, like a bright sun through history and he will remain so forever.

Despite the fact that the infallible imams (A) were created in the highest status of creation, we still read in the salutation of *"Lamentation"*:

". . . after You (Allah) had preconditioned on them (the messengers) the asceticism from the vanities and splendour of this inferior world, and they accepted the conditions and You knew their honesty, and so You accepted them."

Therefore their asceticism was a precondition by Allah the Almighty to accept them even though Allah states in the noble Qur'an:

"Say: Who has forbidden the beautiful (gifts) of Allah, which He has produced for His servants, and the things, clean and pure, (which He has provided) for sustenance?"[72]

Furthermore, the modesty of a leader (and the governing system) saves the country many unnecessary expenses. The wealth and

---

[72] The holy Qur'an: the Ramparts [7]: 32.

51

resources available to the leader does not belong to him, but to the nation.

If the wealth (of a country) was to be passed around between the rulers and they were to use it as they wish and desire - clearly it isn't only ruler but the entire ruling elite and their entourage - there will be none left for the nation. This is clearly observed with despotic regimes in which the ruling dictators use the nation's wealth for their own pleasures, desires and fantasies.

The Imam (A) has been quoted describing the Omayyad rulers as: *"they pass around the wealth of Allah[73] between themselves."*

Abu Tharr (may Allah's mercy be upon him) also described them as: *"those who passed around the wealth of Allah alternatively between themselves."*

Needless to say that one's intrinsic abstention together with the consultation (democratic) process which necessitates the monitoring of rulers by the nation, plus adherence to the guidelines on conduct and expenditure, then the leaders would not be in a position to misuse the wealth of the nation, and therefore meet the needs of the nation.

Although it may be difficult on the body, but abstention from worldly vanities brings about the comfort for the soul just as it provides great pleasures unparalleled by the pleasures of the body.

---

[73] i.e. the public funds.

52

23

Combating Corruption

It is necessary for the Islamic government established in any country to fight corruption in its various forms, such as social and economic corruption as well as corruption in various government offices and the civil service, etc. Corruption causes deterioration and backwardness of the nation after its confidence in the government is lost.

Corruption at the level of government offices and agencies results from bribery, favouritism - patronage and nepotism - and procrastination, which consequently result in wastage of time and wealth. It eventually causes public dismay and, in many cases, leads to the downfall of the government.

Imam Ali has been quoted as saying: *"Four factors contribute to the downfall of governments: Abandoning the principles, Adhering to arrogance, Favouring contemptible individuals and Disposing the praiseworthy".*

He has also been quoted as saying: *"When contemptible individuals or the young and inexperienced are put in charge of government affairs, it will lead to its disintegration and downfall".*

A prominent figure of the Omayyad dynasty was asked for the reason the dynasty fell from grace and government. He replied: "they entrusted major tasks and affairs to the young and inexperienced and assigned minor tasks to prominent figures. Neither the young were competent enough to discharge their duties with respect to the tasks they were assigned, nor the prominent figures carried out their duties because of their disdain and self-esteem . . . and between these two the government was lost.

But why did the Omayyads do that? This is because the young are more susceptible to flattering and obeying orders without questioning whereas the elders are experienced and appreciate the realities and therefore criticise when need be. Hence they removed the elders from major positions and assigned them minor tasks in order to keep them at bay.

This is what we have seen with all despotic regimes, and we saw their disgraceful fall from power. However, if those governments conducted their affairs properly they would have survived many times their lifetime and this is what is expected for the remaining dictators.

As for social and moral corruption, there are issues such as uncontrollable spread of alcohol consumption, gambling, adultery, homosexuality, fraud, deception, lie and defamation, etc.

As for economic corruption: examples are deviation from capitalism such as monopoly, the unbalanced control of the wealth and resources of the nation by a few, improper distribution of the wealth, in a way that the rich die of indigestion and the poor of hunger. Imam Ali (A) is quoted as saying:

"Suffice (for you) your disease of indigestion

While there are around you those who yearn for a portion of meal"

24

Social Reform

As part of its program of reform, the Islamic government must address the issue of social reform. It must amend the sources of deviation and perversion and direct social perversity towards sound and honourable practices by providing righteous environments. For example transforming wine bars and brothels to places of honourable and decent businesses and extricating those in deviation and helping them to become good and useful members of the society.

This means that one may not be prosecuted for practices committed in the past. Furthermore, their practices may not be suspended without providing honourable alternatives, to prevent them from going back to the same practice again.

The prosecution of those who had, in the past, engaged in such practices means the government would fall into the circle of revenge, and we mentioned in a previous section the need for the government to give general amnesty.

On the other hand, if the government bans their practices and abandons them to their affairs without providing honourable alternatives, this would cause increased unemployment. At the same time it would mean a quick return to their previous practices. It is reported that Imam Ali (A) arranged for a prostitute to get married (and lead an honourable life).

Of course such a program of reform is regarded as one of the stages of *"Enjoining and forbidding evil"*.

If the government commissioned a committee to address these issues, it would be possible to rectify them quickly and without further problems.

The same goes for the usury-based banks. The remedy is to change the current system to that based on *Mudahrabah*, and this should be carried out under supervision of a panel of experts in economy as well as religious scholars. To suspend the interest-based banking system at the stroke of a pen and without a careful study and without the provision of a better alternative - such as regulation of the *Mudahrabah* etc. - would result in:

1. Capital drain abroad, which would bring about inflation and its consequences,

2. People withdrawing their assets from the banks leaving the banks, which are important mainstay for the government, with insufficient funds to function. This would in turn result in discontent, which would subsequently undermine the reputation of the government and its economic status.

25

Justice and Equality

Justice is to assign something to its rightful situation, whether in equal ratio or not, and therefore there are a few factors that justice and equality have in common.

For example: a tall and large built person would require four yards of fabric for his garment while a small built person would require less than that. Justice is to give each what they require while this is not equality.

Of course equality must be upheld with respect to general issues such as the judicial system, fines, job opportunities, education, health and other similar issues.

Injustice and inequality, in their respective domains, are the most severe kind of oppression. Oppression could be to oneself or to others and the latter is of greater severity and worse outcome.

People cannot tolerate injustice and inequality as they see themselves - by their nature and rationale - *"equal like the teeth of a comb"* and they see that *"there is no merit for an Arab over non-Arab, nor for a white over a black except for righteousness"*, as reported in the traditions.

And these two issues are rational before they are doctrinal. In fact the Islamic jurisdiction is based on the nature (of mankind) which itself is based on reason. Allah the Almighty states: *"O mankind! We created you from a single (pair) of a male and a female, and made you into nations and tribes, that you may know each other. Verily the most honoured of you in the sight of Allah is (he who is) the most righteous of you. And Allah has full Knowledge and is well-acquainted (with all things)."[74]*

And Imam Ali (A) has been attributed the following poem:

---

[74] The holy Qur'an, the Chambers [49]: 13.

The people are equal in comparison

Their mother is Eve and their father is Adam

Therefore the newly established Islamic government must uphold this Islamic and humanitarian principle with power and resolve, and discharge its duty. In this way it will attract the hearts and minds around to its establishment, which results into more security and more stability.

This is the end of what we wished to state in this book, and Allah is the Facilitator and the Supporter.

Glory be to your Lord, the Lord of Honour and Power! He is beyond what they ascribe (to Him)! And peace be upon the Messengers and Praise to the Lord of the worlds and Blessing of Allah on Muhammad and his purified descendants.

Muhammad Shirazi

The holy City of Qum

5th Rabee' II 1415 Hejri.

Appendix

Grand Ayatollah Mohammad Shirazi's reply
to
the question of a group of Muslims about his views and vision
about the future picture of Iraq[75]

In the name of Allah, the Compassionate, the Merciful

Peace and Blessings of Allah be upon the Muslim brothers.

You have asked about (the situation in) Iraq and the state it must assume in the future after the fall of the current regime by the will of Allah. We shall point to some of the 'aspects' concerned on the basis of Islamic principles, which are in harmony with the human "nature" that is *"the original nature according to which Allah fashioned mankind."*[76]

1. The majority (of the population) must form the ruling government while at the same time the right of minority must be secured. The majority had the greatest role in securing Iraq's freedom on several occasions during this century (20th century). One occasion was the 1920 revolution and the second during the second world war when the religious leaders decreed that the expulsion of the colonial powers from the country was obligatory on everyone. On those occasions the Iraqi nation did not rest until they forced the colonial powers out of the country. On the third occasion it was the majority's

---

[75] Regarding the despot regime in Iraq, Imam Shirazi believes that not only the dictatorial regime must be removed from power but also a fundamental infrastructure must be provided inside the country, which is based on system of consultation, party political pluralism, respect for human right and the right of the minorities.

[76] The holy Qur'an: the Romans [30]: 30.

resistance to the rise of the communism in Iraq . . . and history has recorded those moves in detail.

Furthermore Allah the Almighty has stated in the noble Qur'an:

" . . . who (conduct) their affairs by mutual Consultation . . ."[77] and

" . . . and consult them in affairs (of moment) . . ."[78]

In the holy tradition, it has been reported:

" . . . so that the right of any Muslim individual is not lost."

2. It is essential that the government is supported by constitutional establishments. This must be associated with the provision of freedoms for all groups, associations, and political parties that are not opposed to Islam and the interests of the nation. It is also imperative that there are free elections in the true meaning of the word. Freedom must also be granted for unions, societies, and other similar organisations. There must be freedom of expression in terms of newspapers and other mass media. All the various groups of the society such as workers, farmers, professionals, etc. must be provided with their freedoms. Freedom and dignity of women must also be secured within the framework of Islamic and human rights. In this respect Allah the Almighty has stated in the Qur'an:

" . . . there is no compulsion in religion . . ."[79] and

" . . . He (the Messenger of Allah - Muhammad) releases them (the people) from their heavy burdens and from the yokes that are upon them . . ."[80]

Furthermore Imam Ali (A) is quoted as saying:

"Do not be a slave to others when Allah has created you free."

3. Non-violence should be the general policy for the government's home and foreign affairs as Allah the Almighty has stated:

"O believers enter into peace entirely"[81].

---

[77] The holy Qur'an: Consultation [42]: 38.
[78] The holy Qur'an: the Family of 'Emraan [3]: 159.
[79] The holy Qur'an: the Heifer [2]: 256.
[80] The holy Qur'an: the Heights [7]: 157.
[81] The holy Qur'an: the Heifer [2]: 208.

This is a fundamental principle and any practice to the contrary is exceptional.

4. Human rights must be respected with extreme precision as prescribed by the religion of Islam, which is superior to any human right convention practiced in many countries of the world today. (There is) absolutely no death penalty except if the (leadership) council of religious authorities decrees otherwise (in a specific case). Concerning a particular category of crime or a specific case, if, due to any particular doubt or uncertainty, there was any difference between (the inference and deduction of the relevant rulings of) the members of the council then "*punishments are waived by doubts*"[82].

Also the number of prisoners must be reduced to an absolute minimum, even to a level lower than that internationally accepted today. There can be no torture under any circumstances and absolutely no confiscation of wealth and property.

5. As for past deeds, the principle of "*(Allah) forgives what is past*"[83] must be adhered to, just as the Greatest Messenger (P) pardoned the people of Makkah: "*Go! For you are at liberty.*" as well as pardoning many others. Amir_ol_Mu'meneen (P) also pardoned many people on various occasions. It is evident from reports from Imam Ridha (P) that the application of the *hadeeth* of "*Waive*" to Muslims has a higher priority than to others.

6. The Kurds, Turkmans, and other ethnic groups have all the right to take part in the forthcoming government and the nation. Allah the Almighty has stated:

"*O mankind! We created you from a single (pair) of a male and a female, and made you into nations and tribes, that you may know each other. Verily the most honoured of you in the sight of Allah is the most righteous of you. And Allah has full Knowledge and is well acquainted (with all things).*"[84]

The Messenger of Allah has said:

---

[82] Hurr_Aameli, M.H. "*The Guide to Islamic Law*", vol. 18, p 399. Also in it there is "*Waive the punishments (if there were) uncertainties.*"
[83] The holy Qur'an: Table Spread [5]: 95.
[84] The holy Qur'an: The Apartments [49]: 13.

"There is no merit for an Arab over a non-Arab and not for a red man over a black man except for righteousness."

7. The forthcoming government must adopt the policy of "alliance" or "friendship" with all governments within the framework of the interest of the nation, just as the noble prophet (P) adopted such a policy with various non-Islamic sects including the pagans. The exception to this is aspects such as the occupation of Islamic countries by others as in the case of Palestine and Afghanistan. In this case it is incumbent upon all Muslims to defend (against aggression) since *"(The masses of) the Muslims are like one body. As soon as one organ suffers pain, the rest of the body (organs) would respond through fever and vigil."*

8. In planning the general policy and the broad headlines, the final reference in the constitution of the forthcoming Islamic government in Iraq is the council of jurists or religious authorities, as prescribed by Islam. The noble Messenger (P) said:

"The righteous are masters and the jurists are leaders."

Needless to say the religious authorities would co-operate with the universities for Islamic sciences as well as other professionals and experts in various fields. In fact this is the requisite of consultation and of the council as the Almighty states in the Qur'an:

" . . . and consult them in affairs (of moment) . . ."[85] and

" . . . who (conduct) their affairs by mutual Consultation, . . ."[86]

9. It is imperative upon all Muslims to do all they can to unify all countries of Islam and bring them under one Islamic government as the Almighty states:

"This, your community is a single community and I am your Lord; so worship Me."[87]

The greatest Messenger (P) established the foundation of the single universal government when states unified under the banner of Islam during his lifetime. In this century (20th century) India is an example of this and Europe is working towards such a state.

---

[85] The holy Qur'an: the family of 'Emraan [3]: 159.
[86] The holy Qur'an: Consultation [42]: 38.
[87] The holy Qur'an: The Believers [23]: 52.

Needless to say that disunion of the Islamic states and the existence of geographical borders between them are one of the prime causes of underdevelopment and backwardness. From another angle they are also the causes of conflicts and disputes between them. And from a third viewpoint, such factors bring about the domination of the colonial powers and enable the latter colonise them.

10. The international community must be urged to bring about the necessary pressures on any government that oppresses its own people. Since for a human being, there is no difference between internal oppression (oppression of a government to its own people) and external oppression (state to state oppression), as this is arrived at by reason. Sound reason as well as Islamic jurisdiction does not allow us to let the likes of Mussolini, Hitler and Stalin to do what they like with their people in terms of persecution, forced exile, confiscation and murder under the pretext of "internal affairs". If a nation seeks help from the international community, the latter must provide lawyers and judges to investigate their plight and if there were evidence of oppression (by their own or external government) then they must be rescued from their oppressors.

O Allah, we earnestly request from You an honourable government
through which You strengthen Islam and its people,
and degrade hypocrisy and its followers.
And make us in it amongst the inviters to Your obedience
and the leaders to Your path.
Grant us through it the honour of this world and the hereafter.[88]

---

[88] Supplication of *Eftitah*.

The Author

Ayatollah al-Udhma Imam Muhammad Shirazi is undoubtedly the most eminent *Marje'* or Religious Authority of Muslim world. A charismatic leader who is known for his high moral values, modesty and spirituality, Imam Shirazi is a mentor and a source of aspiration to millions of Muslims; and the means of access to authentic knowledge and teachings of Islam. He has tirelessly devoted himself, and his entire life, to the cause of Islam and Muslims in particular, and to that of mankind in general. He has made extensive contributions in various fields of learning ranging from Jurisprudence and Theology to Government, Politics, Economics, Law, Sociology and Human Rights.

Born in Najaf, Iraq, in 1347 AH, 1928 AD, the young Shirazi continued his studies of different branches of learning under the guidance of various eminent scholars and specialists, as well as his father, the renowned *Marje'* of the time, Ayatollah al-Udhma Mirza Mahdi Shirazi. In the course of his training he showed an outstanding talent and a remarkable appetite for learning as well as a tireless commitment to his work and the cause he believed in. His extraordinary ability, and effort, earned him the recognition at the age of 25, by the *Maraje'* and scholars of the time, of being a *Mujtahid,* a fully qualified religious scholar and lawmaker in the sciences of Islamic jurisprudence and law. He was subsequently able to assume the office of the *Marje'* at the early age of 33 in 1380 AH, 1961.

Imam Shirazi is distinguished for his intellectual ability and holistic vision. He has written various specialized studies that are considered to be among the most important references in the relevant fields. He has enriched the world with his staggering contribution of more than 1000 books, treatise and studies on various branches of learning. His works range from introductory works for the youth to literary and scientific masterpieces. Deeply rooted in the Holy Qur'an and the teachings of the Prophet of Islam, his vision and theories cover such areas as Legislation, Management, Environment, Sociology, Theology, Philosophy, History Human Rights, Law and Islamic beliefs or doctrine. His work on Islamic Jurisprudence (the *al-Fiqh* series) for example constitutes 150 volumes, which run into more than 70,000 pages. Through his original thoughts and ideas he has championed the causes of issues such as the family, human rights, freedom of expression, political pluralism, non-violence, and Shura or consultative system of leadership.

Throughout his life, because of his total dedication to the Teachings of Islam, and because of his views on various issues, which are based on those teachings, he came under sustained pressure from the authorities in Iraq as well as in Iran. His views on, and his call for issues such as freedom of expression, party political pluralism, peace and non-violence brought about the wrath of the authorities in Iran. His uncompromising stance on implementing the teachings of Islam in all aspects of government including such vital matters as leadership by consensus or *Showral-Foqaha'-al-Maraje'* (religious authorities' council of leadership) attracted the fury of those at the helm.

He was therefore forced into house arrest for more than twenty years. His staff, followers, and family members were subjected to continued harassment, arbitrary arrest and torture.

Having spent the entire of his adult life striving for the greater enlightenment of the Muslims and mankind, Imam Shirazi died in suspicious circumstances in the holy city of Qum, Iran, on Monday the 2nd Shawwal 1422 AH, 17th December 2001. More than half a million people attended his funeral procession the following day.

Imam Shirazi believed in the fundamental and elementary nature of freedom in mankind. He used to call for freedom of expression, political plurality, debate and discussion, tolerance and forgiveness.

He strongly believed in the consultative system of leadership and calls for the establishment of the leadership council of religious authorities. He continuously called for the establishment of the universal Islamic government to encompass all the Muslim countries. These and other ideas are discussed in detail in his books of more than 1000.

Other Publications by *fountain books*

www.fountainbooks.com

1.   Fundamentals of Islam

In this book the author outlines the five fundamental principles of Islam, namely *Tawheed* (the Indivisible Oneness of God), *Adl* (Divine Justice), *Nubowwah* (Prophethood), *Imamah* (Leadership of mankind), and *Me'ad* (Resurrection). For each principle, the author presents a brief, and to the point, discussion on the significance of the issue concerned. The book could serve as a good introduction to Islamic beliefs.

2.   Islamic Beliefs for All

In this book the author discusses the five fundamental principles of Islam. These principles are *Tawheed* or the Indivisible Oneness of God, *Adl* or Divine Justice, Prophethood, *Imamah* or the Leadership of mankind after the prophet, and Resurrection. What distinguish this book are the author's subtle approach in addressing the issues concerned and the simple examples given to illustrate the discussion. This authoritative work is not only important to Muslims, but it would also be of interest to those non-Muslims who seek to explore Islam and its doctrine. This easy to read book would be a valuable reference for Religious Education.

3.   What is Islam? An introduction to principles and beliefs

Few would dare to attempt to summarize the Islamic faith in a book of this size but this is the aim of the late Grand Ayatollah Muhammad al-Shirazi, one of the most eminent Islamic authorities of modern times. Eschewing complicated jargon and deliberately using succinct and lucid language within a "question and answer" format, he has sought to convey the richness and profound spirituality of the Islamic message in all its aspects to the widest possible audience. There are necessarily some Arabic and technical terms but these have been kept to a minimum. The late Sayyid Shirazi covers all the main aspects of Islam, from the fundamental beliefs such as the Oneness of God and His justice and prophethood to topics like ablutions, praying, fasting, and making the Hajj and also deals with such diverse subjects as Islamic law, economics, politics, the Islamic view of society, the issue of freedom in Islam, and so on. This is a book which will not only be useful for Muslims who want to find out more about their religion but also for non-Muslims who seek a concise introduction to what Islam is all about.

4.   The Family

In this book the author highlights the problems he sees both in Islamic societies and in west societies today that arise from the phenomenon of unmarried young men and women, through to birth control and contraception. He surveys the idea of marriage in various religions and schools of thought, and discusses polygamy from the Islamic perspective. As well as being a call to the Muslim world to revert to the true teachings of Islam, this book can also be of use as an introduction to others who seek some answers to the social problems of today. This is because Islam provides detailed teachings that promise success in every area of human life on individual and societal levels, and furthermore the practicality and success of those teachings have been proven in the course of history.

5.   The Qur'an: When was it compiled?

In this book the author addresses the issues of when the Holy Qur'an was compiled, on what and whose instructions was this task carried out, and who accomplished its compilation in the form that it is available today.   In this work the author presents undisputable evidence as to address these crucial questions.   Through historical, methodical and logical analyses, the author establishes how and when the compilation of the Holy Qur'an was achieved.   In the latter half of the book the author cites many Prophetic traditions (*hadith*) on the significance of the learning and recitation of Holy Qur'an.   It is a must read for every Muslim, and any non-Muslim who follows Islamic issues.

6.   War, Peace and Non-violence: An Islamic perspective

In this work the author addresses three controversial issues, which have come to be associated with Islam.   Through his extensive knowledge of the teachings of Islam, the author presents the Islamic stand on war, peace and non-violence, as found in the traditions and teachings of the Prophet of Islam, which could serve as exemplary models for the Mankind.   Detailed accounts of the traditions of Prophet in his dealings with his foes during war or peace times are presented in this book, which gives the reader a clear insight into the way and the basis upon which the Prophet of Islam used to conduct his affairs in this respect.

7.   Islamic System of Government

In this introductory book the author outlines the basic principles of a government based on the teachings of Islam. The author begins with the aim and objectives of the government according to Islam and the extent of its authority in that framework. He then addresses, from the Islamic viewpoint, the significance and fundamental nature of such issues as consultative system of government, judicial system, freedoms, party political pluralism, social justice, human rights, foreign policy, etc.   The author also outlines the policies of a government on issues such as education, welfare, health, crime, services, etc. as well as such matters as the government's income, and authority.

8.   The Bible and Christianity: an Islamic view

In this work the author carries out a brief investigation into the Bible and presents his findings. They show that some of the most noble men, i.e. the Prophets, who have been chosen by God Almighty as His messengers to mankind, are accused in the Bible to have committed some of the most vile and immoral conducts known to man. Prophets are accused of deception, lying, fornication, rape, incest, murder, and the list goes on. Even God does not escape unscathed in the Bible . . . false characteristics are attributed to Him, or He is accused of making His messengers to commit foul acts.

In the second part of this work the author presents some of the debates he had with the Christians who visited him in his residence in Karbala, Iraq. The debates concerned their impression of Islam and its doctrine as well as their own religious beliefs. In this presentation the author shows how he invited non-Muslims to Islam through calm but rational and intellectual debates with them. The book makes an interesting read, especially when the reader can see the simple arguments put forward in these debates.

9.   The Guide to Hajj Rites

This handbook is a comprehensive but easy to follow book that guides the reader through all the stages of the Hajj pilgrimage. It addresses all aspects of the Hajj program and the rites that must be observed. It is a must for anyone who intends to go to the Hajj pilgrimage

10. *The Rights of Prisoners according to Islamic teachings*

In general, Islam considers imprisonment as a case of last resort in many circumstances, however, according to Islamic teachings there are only a few offences that would lead to imprisonment. Under non-Islamic system, of course the offender should be reprimanded, but any chastisement prescribed by Islamic teachings may only be implemented if all the relevant criteria and the preconditions prescribed are also met. If the criteria are not met, then the prescribed punishment may not be executed.

In this book the author addresses such issues as the fundamental nature of freedom, the rights of prisoner, and the harmful effects of imprisonment on the individual concerned as well as on society, and the kind of offences that would lead to imprisonment under an Islamic system. The author also cites a few cases to demonstrate the attitude the Islamic ruler should take towards offence; to try to find reasons to waive the punishments in any particular case. The author also addresses the issue of torture in general, and mental and physical ill treatment that is carried out under the guise of interrogation and extracting confession from a detainee or a suspect.

This brief work presents the teachings of Islam with respect to the rights of those when imprisoned, and shows that the teachings of Islam are designed, by the designer and maker of mankind, for the benefit of mankind wherever he may be.

11. *Husayn - The Sacrifice for Mankind*

This is a collection of articles about a totally unique individual who, through his remarkable sacrifices, managed to change the course of history and the direction that mankind was heading for. He is none other than Husayn, the grandson of the Prophet of Islam, Muhammad, and the second son of Fatima and Ali, peace be upon them. Imam Husayn peace be upon him stood up to tyranny and oppression and gave everything he had, including his life and the lives of his most beloved sons and brothers as well as those of his closest allies, in order to awaken the masses, reform society and rectify the distortion that has been inflicted on Islam.

The articles in this work cover some aspects of the aims and objectives of Imam Husayn's movement, the difference between his strategy and that of his brother Imam Hasan in facing tyranny and despotism, the examples he set, and the lessons that are learnt from the events that lead up to Karbala fourteen centuries ago. Besides the benefits of his movement, the personality of Imam Hussain peace be upon him as reflected by the many hadith and teachings of Prophet Muhammad is also discussed. Also included in this work are a number of questions and answers about the commemoration ceremonies observed by the Muslims around the world on the occasion of Ashura.

12. Aspects of the Political Theory of Imam Shirazi

Muhammad G. Ayub is a well-known Islamist political activist within the Iraqi circle who has established a long history of political struggle over the past three decades. He was attracted by the views of the Imam Muhammad Shirazi in the fields of social and political sciences. This prompted the author to write this book to introduce the reader to these views that have remained relatively unknown amongst Muslim activists and reformists. It covers such aspects on politics as freedom of expression, party-political pluralism and organisation, social justice, peace and non-violence, human rights, consultation system of government, etc.